SCHOLASTIC SCIENCE READERS™

LEVEL
1
AGES 5 AND 6

P9-DTA-693

SPIDERS

Carolyn B. Otto

SCHOLASTIC
REFERENCE

PHOTO CREDITS: Cover: Christoph Burki/Tony Stone Images. Page 1: Brian Kenney; 3: Pal Hermansen/Tony Stone Images; 4: Christoph Burki/Tony Stone Images; 5: Bob Gossington/Bruce Colman; 6: Dwight Kuhn; 7: Robert and Linda Mitchell; 8: Dwight Kuhn; 9, top: Robert and Linda Mitchell; 9, bottom: Brian Kenney; 10, top: Dwight Kuhn; 10, bottom: Robert and Linda Mitchell; 11, top: Dwight Kuhn; 11, bottom: Robert and Linda Mitchell; 12: Brian Kenney; 13: Robert and Linda Mitchell; 15: Robert and Linda Mitchell; 16: Robert and Linda Mitchell; 17: Nuridsany & Perennou/Photo Researchers; 18: Robert and Linda Mitchell; 19: Tom Bean/Tony Stone Images; 20: Robert and Linda Mitchell; 21: Robert and Linda Mitchell; 22: Robert and Linda Mitchell; 23: Robert and Linda Mitchell; 25: Dwight Kuhn; 26: Dwight Kuhn; 29: Dwight Kuhn; 30: Robert and Linda Mitchell.

Library of Congress Cataloging-in-Publication Data available.

ISBN 0-439-38245-9

Book design by Barbara Balch and Kay Petronio
Photo research by Sarah Longacre

10 9 8 7 6 5   03 04 05

Printed in the U.S.A. 23

First trade printing, October 2002

We are grateful to Francie Alexander, reading specialist, and to Adele M. Brodkin, Ph.D., developmental psychologist, for their contributions to the development of this series.

Our thanks also to our science consultant
Dr. Michael L. Draney, University of Wisconsin–Green Bay.

Spiders live all over the world.

3

Spiders live all around
you. Spiders might live in
a garden.

They might live in
your house.

When you find a spider,
it is better not to touch it.

Some spiders bite. And most have **venom** (**ven**-uhm). But most spiders will not hurt you.

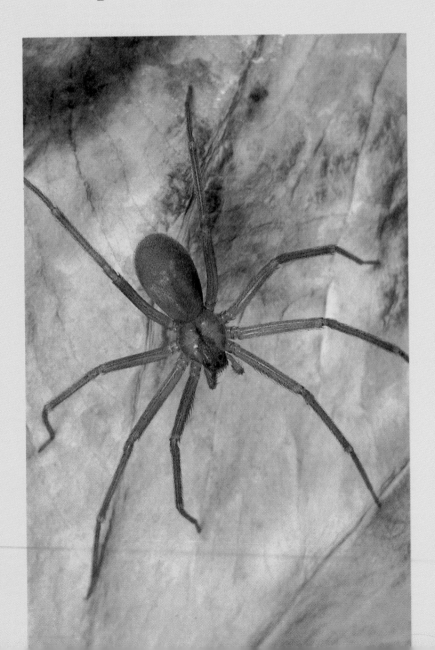

So when you find a spider,
just look at that spider closely.
Spiders are very interesting!

Spiders can
be big, but
never as big
as you are.

Most spiders
are small.
Some are so
tiny you can
hardly see
them.

Some spiders
are brown
and hairy. Some
are yellow.

Some are
green. Spiders
come in many
colors!

There are lots of different
kinds of spiders.

Spiders have two main parts to their bodies. They have eight legs.

Most spiders have eight eyes, too. But some spiders have six eyes, or four eyes, or two eyes. Some spiders live in dark caves and don't have eyes at all!

All spiders make **silk**. Spiders use silk in different ways.

Some spiders use silk to build their homes. This spider has a home under the ground.

This spider has a home
under the water.

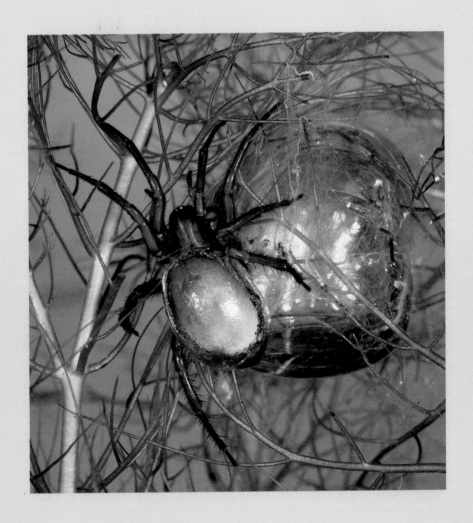

Many spiders use silk to build **webs**. Different kinds of spiders build different kinds of webs. They build webs in different shapes.

This web is called an orb web. Orb is another word for circle. The spider who made it is waiting to catch a meal.

Orb web >

This spider has caught a grasshopper in her web. She wraps the grasshopper in threads of silk. The spider will eat the grasshopper later.

Take a Closer Look

A grasshopper caught in silk threads

Spiders often use silk to protect their eggs. There are many eggs in this **egg sac**. So, there will be lots of baby spiders.

Take a Closer Look

A spider with her egg sac

This spider carries her babies
on her back. The babies hold
on tightly. They are not ready
to leave their mother.

These baby spiders are
ready to go. They spin a long
thread of silk. The silk helps
carry them up in the air.

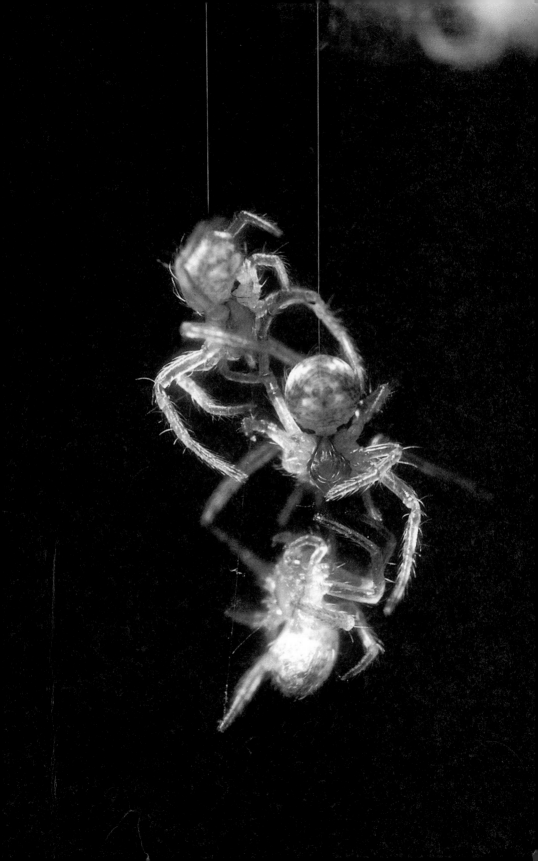

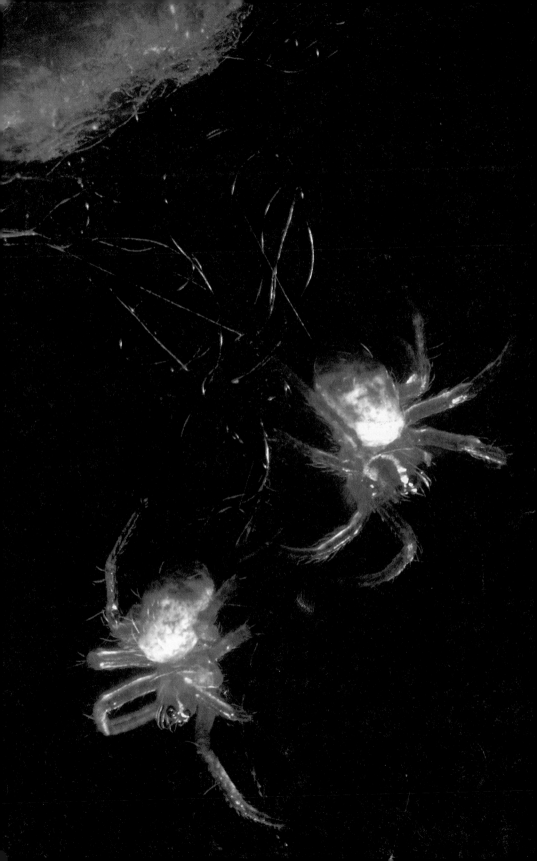

The baby spiders will float in the air. Some babies will land nearby. Others will land much farther away. They will all begin new lives on their own.

If you see a spider, remember to look and learn. Try to see what that spider is doing. Think about where the spider came from.

It may have come from
far away, floating on a thread
of silk.

Glossary

egg sac—a silk covering to protect a spider's eggs

silk—the thin threads spiders make

venom (**ven**-uhm)—poison used to kill or quiet prey

webs—traps made of silk to catch food

A Note to Parents

Learning to read is such an exciting time in a child's life. You may delight in sharing your favorite fairy tales and picture books with your child.

But don't forget the importance of introducing your child to the world of nonfiction. The ability to read and comprehend factual material will be essential to your child in school, and throughout life. The Scholastic Science Readers™ series was created especially with beginning readers in mind. These books, with their clear texts and beautiful photographs, will help you to share the wonders of science with *your* new reader.

Suggested Activity

Help your child make his or her own spiderweb out of string or thread! Obtain a non-splintery, square shaped piece of wood—pine is good—from a lumberyard, or left over from another woodworking project. Carefully pound five or six 1½ inch nails into the surface of the wood in a circular pattern, securing them but allowing them to extend about 1 inch above the surface of the wood. Use caution, and be sure that the nails don't poke through to the other side of the wood. Your child can wind string or thread around the nails to create a beautiful web, modeled after the many webs he or she has seen in this book and in your neighborhood.